Mindfulness

Mindful Eating

Proven Secrets to Lose Weight, Stop Overeating and Feel Relaxed

By Maya Faro

Copyright Maya Faro© 2016

All rights reserved. No part of this publication may be reproduced, stored in a retrieval system, or transmitted, in any form or by any means, electronic, mechanical, photocopying, recording or otherwise, without the prior written permission of the author and the publishers.

The scanning, uploading, and distribution of this book via the Internet or via any other means without the permission of the author is illegal and punishable by law. Please purchase only authorized electronic editions, and do not participate in or encourage electronic piracy of copyrighted materials.

Maya Faro © Copyright 2016 - All rights reserved.

Legal Notice:

This book is copyright protected. It for personal use only.

Disclaimer Notice:

Please note the information contained in this document is for educational and entertainment purposes only. Every attempt has been made to provide accurate, up to date and completely reliable information. No warranties of any kind are expressed or implied.

Readers acknowledge that the author is not engaging in the rendering of legal, financial, medical or professional advice. By reading this document, the reader agrees that under no circumstances are we responsible for any losses, direct or indirect, which are incurred as a result of the use of information contained within this document, including, but not limited to, errors, omissions, or inaccuracies.

Contents

Letter from the Author 6
Chapter 1 – The Joy of Mindfulness.. 9
   What is Mindfulness Anyway?.. 9
   The Important connection with Emotions. 10
   Other benefits of Mindfulness and meditation 12
   Spiritual Awakening... 12
   Emotional Healing 12
   Best Mindfulness Tip 13
Chapter 2. How to be Mindful 14
   Taking it further 16
   Best Mindfulness Tips.. 18
   Mindful Expressions to Experiment with.............................. 20
Chapter 3 - The Fascinatingly Complex Business of Food and Eating 20
   Fact Number 1. 21
   Fact Number 2.. 22
   Transforming your relationship with food. 23
   Top Mindfulness Tip 25
Chapter 4 The Core Wound of Worthlessness 27
   Learning Some More... 29
   Emotional Hunger 30
   Top Mindfulness Tips 31
Chapter 5 Transforming the Cycle of Emotional Eating............ 34
   See if you recognize any of these emotions in yourself 35
   Alternative Ways to Manage these Emotions....................... 36
   Top Mindfulness Tips 40

Chapter 6 - Mindful Eating in a Mindful Life 42
   Mindful Eating 43
   Best Mindful Tip 49

Chapter 7 - Mindfulness and Health 50
   What Else will Help to Boost Both yourHealth and your Mindfulness? 51

Chapter 8- Living the Mindful Life 59
   Being mindful about the origin of your food 59
   Taking it a little further 61
   Mindful eating and the Planet 62

Conclusion 63

Letter from the Author

Mindfulness is very much in favor at the moment. It's used in schools, homes and businesses as one of the most successful ways to deal with everyday stressors. In a stress-filled society, this makes a lot of sense. However, for those of us who enter the mindfulness practices through the door of 'stress management,' we quickly discover that there is much more to it than making it easier for us to deal with our anxiety and high blood pressure! It can take us on a healing journey to an awakening to the great beauty of life and the joy it is to be part of it.

My journey with Mindfulness began with being a real Type A personality; being driven to succeed, and to succeed fast. My first toe-dip into the strange world of 'calmness' and 'centredness' came from starting yoga lessons in the hope that I would learn how to relax. The yoga teacher introduced me to meditation in one of the classes and having read a few articles on the uses of meditation for stress management in typical Type A style I thought it would be a good idea to learn meditation too. So off I went to those classes as well. Of course, I had no time to do these given my driven and accelerating career – but I managed to squeeze in a few sessions with the local TM teacher. I'd been ticking the boxes about doing the right things - but my drivenness was still in charge, and I felt frustrated when my blood pressure stayed a little too high and my anxiety levels didn't change.

But a strange thing happened. That little voice inside we sometimes get kept telling me that mindful meditation was important, and I kept practicing it. This went on for years – and I never really got into meditation in the way that authors wrote about their experience with meditation. I was so jealous of them, and my relationship with meditation was one of complete failure! Even more frustrating, as you can imagine. But I didn't stop. I pared the daily time I gave 'sitting there' with my mind whirling about right down to 5 minutes every day – but I didn't stop!

Somewhere along the way, I got interested in why on earth I couldn't relax, focus, be calm and do all those good things. This happened around the time when my weight began to get out of control as I snacked as I ran, never stopped for breakfast or lunches, then stuffed myself in the evenings before falling into bed in a big heap. As I bought my latest power suit and realized that I had gone up 2 dress sizes in the last year, I suddenly wondered if there was a connection between the relaxation issue and the eating/weight issue. Duh! Of course, there was. They were the symptoms of a big issue I had with my own worth (well... lack of worth, actually).

One day that little voice spoke up again, and it said in no uncertain terms – "be here, NOW." No matter how much I distracted myself with work, food, travel, films, my mind kept telling me to STOP. Look around, use my senses – walk out of the past and my regrets and the self-beating I gave myself, -walk out of the future where everything I couldn't control lived and fed my fears and actually live in the present. Radical!

I'd arrived at Mindfulness.

My journey to it and with it was long, and I am still on this journey today. I hope to give you some shortcuts, some perspectives, some principles and some practices that will make it easier for you than I made it for myself. Enjoy the read. Keep an open mind and take the time to get REALLY interested in yourself and your life. You are worth it.

Chapter 1 – The Joy of Mindfulness

"Feelings come and go like clouds in a windy sky. Conscious breathing is my anchor."
― *Thich Nhat Hanh*

What is Mindfulness Anyway?

Mindfulness is a behavior we can learn to help us in some odd moments of a challenging day. It is also potentially a central part of a way of life that can transform you from a somewhat unhappy, struggling person to someone who is usually happy and optimistic and can handle the pains, pangs, and joy of living well. Truly!

There is some general confusion about mindfulness and meditation which it is helpful to clear up first. Meditation is a practice where you set some time aside to focus quietly. The purpose is to do something positive for yourself by connecting with yourself again and centering so that you can become calm with a clear mind. Mindfulness is expressly about focusing on the present moment. It is one style of meditation, and that is where the confusion has arisen.

Many people use the words interchangeably, and maybe that doesn't matter as the point of all the other types of meditation and of mindfulness itself, is to bring us to a place of happiness and reality. A place where we are accepting of Life as it is.

The Important connection with Emotions.

"Feelings come and go like clouds…." Says Thich Naht Hanh

The rise in interest and use of mediation has been meteoric in the last twenty years. As the number of stressors in our lives has grown with the multiple forms of communication available and financial demands, have increased with recessions and money market volatility, more doctors are prescribing 'meditation' as a stress management tool. It is a healthier option than Valium! It helps us manage that swirling soup of emotion and unhelpful behaviors and habits we have developed to help us cope.

However it isn't an easier option for it requires commitment and practice, and that is where many people give up. Ironically in a life that has so many demands, when they most need to slow down and center, they say they have no time to do the practice! However for those who do take their quality of life and their health seriously, it is a commitment that has quite amazing results.

One of the very common difficulties people have with stress management is actually not with the stressors themselves. It is with their emotional management as their levels of anxiety, fear, frustration or overwhelm take over and they can't find beneficial ways to control these feelings. They then begin to sublimate them; distract themselves, eat more, develop addictive behaviors, turn to comfort food, nicotine, alcohol... as an attempt to distance themselves from their very uncomfortable feelings.

When we are in the grip of an emotional state, it seems to take us over, and we start to think that the feeling is what we are. "I'm so frustrated I could scream." "I'm anxious all the time." It becomes very difficult to recognize that these are temporary emotions which are blocking our capacity to think and listen. And that, in fact., we have a very creative mind which could problem solve the situation pretty well if we could get it to be clear enough to start working.

And this is where meditation comes in. Through taking up one of the forms of mediation such as TM (Transcendental Meditation), Insight Mediation, Walking Mediation, Zen Meditation…. or Mindfulness Mediation we can start to quieten down. This means we can still our crazy 'monkey mind,' listen to the intuitive voice inside and separate ourselves out from the emotional turmoil caused by too many stress hormones. We can begin to think again.

Other benefits of Mindfulness and meditation

Spiritual Awakening

There are other reasons to meditate, not only to help with stress management. For thousands of years, people have used meditation as a pathway to Awakening themselves spiritually. Buddhists have been using Mindful Mediation for centuries and Thich Nhat Hahn, a modern Buddhist monk, has brought the practice to the Western world in a very accessible way.   For those of you who have an interest in this pathway and strive to live in a way that keeps you connected with the Divine, Mindfulness practice is a very lovely method of being open to life, glorying in the beauty of it and living every moment fully and authentically.

Emotional Healing

Sadly many people have experienced some kind of trauma in their lives or have struggled with the pain of emotions that they cannot get away from such as shame, guilt, severe anxiety. Sometimes these emotional states have lead to mental health issues such as depression. For people in that kind of state, the practice of mindfulness meditation can be a lifeline. It sets up conditions in the mind, body, and soul that allow the person to enter the trauma or the pain equipped to manage it differently and better.

Used in this way Mindfulness is a very powerful healer and is particularly effective used in conjunction with psychotherapy or counseling so that the person can make sense of what is happening.

Best Mindfulness Tip

Let's turn to one of the most influential and respected Zen Buddhist monks of our time, Thich Nhat Hanh, and take inspiration from what he says about mindful living. This is taken from his books on "The Art of Mindful Living".

"Mindfulness is the capacity to be aware of what is going on and what is there. The object of your mindfulness can be anything." We are always aware – in fact, we are awareness itself.

Thich Nhat Hanh carries on, "You can look at the sky, breathe in, and say:

"Breathing in, I am aware of the blue sky." Then you can add "With each breath I come back to the present moment."

Chapter 2. How to be Mindful

Ok. So let's take it at a practical level first. Mindfulness is a behavior we can learn. Which is great because it is not a difficult skill. It is not likely that we pay much attention to 'living in the present' left to our own devices. There are too many distractions and habits of mind and body that get in the way.

But what we can do is begin to intentionally practice 'stopping' from time to time and just paying attention to 'what is'. 'What is' might be:

* the air quality around us,

*a beautiful view in front of us,

* the aroma of bread baking,

* soulful music exquisitely played,

* the sun playing on leaves and dappling the ground in front of us

* a traffic jam,

* the noise of people shouting,

* the sound of a school playground at break time

*the jostle of people rushing by,

* police sirens blaring…. So many things can be part of the present moment.

Notice how we called upon the senses to help bring us into the present. The senses are an excellent place to start 'stopping'.

The next thing to notice once we have checked in with our senses and observed what is making the most impact on us is to switch off the part of our mind that jumps in with judgments about 'what is.' It's too much, it's beautiful, but it won't last, if I don't stop smelling that bread I'll go and buy some and get fat, people are so rude.... This is another list that can go on and on and turn our mood sour and negative in no time.

To keep off the 'monkey mind' chatter, especially the judgmental stuff, the next step is to open those senses wide and notice things you may not have picked up on in the first sweep. Keep it non-judgemental. Just notice.

For many people at the start of their mindfulness practice, this is a good place to stop. You will have given yourself a few moments of quietness, tuned into the very immediate present and interrupted the stream of negative, criticisms you may be in the habit of hearing. This alone will change your experience of you day if you stop to do this a few times. Maybe aim for 3 'stops' per day at first.

That small process is a Mindful everyday practice. The object you are aware of can change – it can be your heart, your breath, the kaleidoscope of color around you, a person passing.... Just look around right now – stop reading. What are you aware of?

Taking it further

A favorite place for mindful meditators is the' inside'. This is where they tune into their feelings, their inner self-talk, the sensations in their body below the level of the usual senses as you did above. Then you can turn your awareness inside. Is your tummy rumbling, are there sounds humming in your ears? Is there an ache you hadn't noticed before when you were busy? Are you thirsty? Can you feel the beating of your heart? What is that 'mind monkey' of yours telling you now? What beliefs are you running as you jump to judgment (especially about yourself)? Whatever is happening practice smiling at it gently and imagine putting it on a cloud and letting it go.

This extension of the mindfulness practice is something you can add to what you did in the last section, or it can be a new practice you experiment with. It's your choice. Just notice what feels easy and positive for you.

Finally, we intentionally, open up our awareness again and scan what is present noticing what we feel appreciation for. We can be aware of the things we picked up on already and send them our appreciation through our thoughts/imagination. Or we can look around anew and notice more subtle things such as picturing all the people who were involved in putting up the traffic lights to ensure our safety at danger spots – even though that was done years ago. Or we can be aware of the warmth of the sun, the softness of the rain, the wonder of human senses being able to take all this in. Appreciate yourself for stopping. Thank yourself for appreciating! And if you can find compassion in there as well as you notice the people rushing and jostling around you, send then send your compassion to them too.

So, you see, in just a pause of a few seconds so much is right there in your present that you tend to miss with your constant focus on the past and the future. As humans locked into old habits of thinking, we tend to spend a lot of time in the past, regretting some things that happened, feeling guilt, shame or rage about them, telling ourselves stories to try to make sense of why they happened... Using up a lot of our attention on things we cannot change. Alternatively, we spend much time in the future. We anticipate what could happen, the worst that could happen, the least that could happen and take up a great deal of time, energy and attention being anxious.   Again we are spending our precious life attending to things that cannot be predicted.

 Imagine taking it step by step, practicing being attentive to one aspect at a time until, after a while, you realize that you don't look at the world the same way anymore, that you are calm, centered and interested in things (including yourself) instead of hassled, critical and scattered.   At that point, you will recognize that you have transformed your whole life.

Best Mindfulness Tips

1. One of the most useful mindfulness techniques is that of following the breath. It is always with you and acts as a bridge between body and mind, inside and outside. You never have to turn your awareness far away if you just seek your breath.

    Learning to come into the present by feeling for your breath then turning your awareness onto it and noticing how long your in-breath is, and how long your out-breath is will calm and center you quickly. You may even notice those tiny, profoundly silent pauses just after your in-breath is full, and just after your out-breath is empty. In doing this, you will focus your concentration on the WHOLE breath, and your concentration will improve, as well as your capacity to stay mindfully exactly in the present moment.

You can also add a smile to your out breath. "As I breathe in I am aware of...... as I breathe out, I smile."

Doing this small thing frequently during the day takes you away from the past and the future and deposits you firmly in the present. Where life indeed is a present (gift) once, we develop the habit of awareness.

2. If you would like to have alternatives to your breath as the anchors for your attention, then the following are all useful.
   - Blue sky
   - Heartbeat
   - The happiness you feel right now
3. Although the next practice is not strictly mindfulness it is one which can and does, change your life. Buddha is quoted as *saying " When words are both true and kind, they can change our world."* Buddha.

Loving kindness is a part of the mindful, meditative tradition in Buddhism and so getting into the habit of saying to yourself, and others, these expressions you will find that your sense of openness, humility, authenticity and honesty are increased. These attributes tend to make you more approachable and human to other people, drawing them to you because it is so rare to find someone who will be straight forward and open.

Mindful Expressions to Experiment with

I don't know

I was wrong

I made a mistake

It happens

How can I help?

Chapter 3 - The Fascinatingly Complex Business of Food and Eating

"Letting go gives us freedom and freedom is the only condition for happiness."
— Thich Nhat Hanh

Having begun to learn the practice of mindfulness let's look at Food and Eating now as we move towards combining mindfulness with eating in one beautiful process.

Fact Number 1.

We can't do without Food.

The trouble with Food is also the wonderfulness of it too. The fact is, we can't do without food. We came into the world needing food so the hunger to eat to nourish ourselves is a very deeply rooted instinct. Right from the moment of birth when we sought food to replenish our strength from the birthing process and build our strength to mature we began to associate food with survival and satisfaction. We came to link it to a feeling of being secure and replete and comfortable. This is very powerful psychological stuff.

It means that right from the word go we associated our eating with a very positive emotional state. Even more complex is that we associated it with being safe. Our bodies and brains are wired to make sure we are secure; if we are not safe, we will feel afraid as a constant reminder to do something about our state. For many people feeling a state of fear gets muddled up in their minds and they seek for food to try to get themselves balanced again. It all happened so long ago when our brains were immature that untangling to the point at which we got muddled up is impossible. So, we keep reaching for food even if we are just a bit scared of going to the dentist, and it is nothing to do with not being safe.

Fact Number 2.

We muddle up emotions that are to do with something else into the experience of eating food.

This complicated mess in our minds can gradually take over if our childhood held many challenges for us and slowly but steadily we begin to have a very complex relationship with food. It can lead to us compulsively eating, eating for comfort, eating when we are scared, eating when we have any kind of uncomfortable emotion.... It can also lead us to refuse food to gain a sort of control, or to show a deep loss and reflect an emptiness inside. Any of these can become a lifelong pattern. Food becomes a substitute, a friend, a thing at never lets you down, it always there, it is what we cling to – or push away.

At that point, a vicious cycle starts to happen as we feel unhappy and self-critical about our weight, our shape and our lack of control. Being in that miserable emotional state triggers the desire for food or the rejection of it. For instance, it can encourage us to eat again, and we succumb 'just this once.' But the self-critical part of us jumps in again and starts to beat us up, telling us how bad we are, how we'll regret it, how we should know better. It's a very vicious cycle!

Transforming your relationship with food.

The splendid news is that changing your relationship with food is entirely possible. The less good news – albeit, very honest, is that it is a process. It was a process that took place over a long time that got you to the point of using food as a substitute and support for all kinds of situations and emotions. And it is a process over time that will take us out.

So this means that we will need patience and time. However, two other attributes will make the transformation of that relationship with food a success. These are kindness and curiosity.

Kindness.

Another way people talk about mindfulness is by describing it as 'loving-kindness'. By this, they mean that as you observe the world as it is right now, this minute, you do so with an attitude of compassion. Or put another way 'lovingly and kindly'. So, as you begin to observe your patterns of eating and your relationship with food you approach this and yourself with softness and love.

Why does kindness work? First, because, for most of us, our inner Critic is very active and our inner Child is given a steady stream of judgment and unkindness. Just like any child, we need compassion and understanding from someone else to help us out of that pit of self-hatred. In fact, for many people 'self-hatred' is too soft a term and what they report feeling is actually 'self-loathing.' This is pretty horrible for anyone who feels this way. Starting to just be a little more gentle with the judgment would be an excellent way to begin using mindfulness to help you understand the muddled bits inside about what food has come to mean to you over and above being something that fuels you for the day.

Curiosity

This is another extremely helpful attribute to cultivate and an active part of mindfulness. It is an entirely natural human trait – we are wired to try to make sense out of the world, and this is a very useful way to learn how to take a step back when you are observing yourself and your reactions to food and eating. There is no judgment in this curiosity. This is just like being a scientist wondering what is making something happen and watching the process to that they can learn and understand it.

So when we begin to blend kindness, compassion, interest and love as we watch ourselves act in different ways a new dynamic is set up inside. From that stream of criticism and judgment, the inner Child used to with and drown under its deluge, a fresh stream of kind mindfulness bring relief and growth.

In that atmosphere the inner You can begin to peer out from behind walls of shame, guilt and fear and start to grow in understanding. With that comes an even greater curiosity as we find ourselves and our behavior increasingly fascinating. Gaining that distance from ourselves as we practice mindfulness around food and eating allows changes in the relationship with food to emerge.

Top Mindfulness Tip

"Sometimes your joy is the source of your smile, but sometimes your smile can be the source of your joy." — Thich Nhat Hanh

Bring your mind to your face and lips and feel for the shape of your smile. If you are not smiling, bring a softening to your lips and let them very gently curve. Allow a sense of kind acceptance to flow from that gentle smile and let it spread out to whoever might see it.

In a back to front way feeling yourself smile changes your level of happiness. You never need to depend on something outside you being the cause of your happiness again.

Chapter 4 The Core Wound of Worthlessness

"You are breathing in, and while breathing in, you know that you are alive." Thich Nhat Hanh

Before we can look at some lovely every day mindful practices where you can combine mindfulness with eating, we need to look at some more of the psychological aspects of our mind, eating, and food.

For most people just enjoying the practice of noticing their food and their process of eating will be enough to take them happily into the world of mindfulness and meditation. But for some that 'complicated relationship with food' takes up a larger part of their attention and they might want to use Mindful Eating as a way to heal the relationship. If you are one of the millions of people who have a challenging relationship with food – this next section may resonate with you!

Self-esteem

One of the current American spiritual teachers, Adyashanti, talks about the 'core wound of unworthiness' being a Western disease and says that the sense of being unworthy is embedded deep in our psyches for many reasons. This is such an undermining state of affairs that it is no wonder that so many of us turn to food/overwork/ alcohol/drugs/sex for comfort and security to try to escape that feeling of worthlessness.

According to Adyashanti mindfulness meditation is one of the most effective ways of healing that wound. The process of loving kindness and attention to oneself and the world starts to open up joy and appreciation of life itself. With that comes the recognition that self-esteem (worthiness) does not depend on your behavior at all. It is entirely about being a human being and that that, in itself, is what gives you value. It doesn't depend on merit or reward, on eating or not eating, on being cruel or being kind. You discover you have value because you 'are'; you are here, now, this minute taking part in Life.

Apart from the general, cultural epidemic of 'unworthiness' talked of by Adya you are likely to make the discovery as you get into the practice of gentle, kind and curious mindfulness around your relationship with food that your sense of self-worth is very low. This is an uncomfortable state to be in as it gets in the way of so many things. Typically it stops you taking up opportunities that come your way. The voice inside that is so full of self-doubt makes you too cautious to try something new, in case you fail. This constant feeling of not being good enough, not being able to take on challenges can become a stress trigger for eating. This, in turn, leads to another wave of self-hate and more internal criticism. This is a vicious cycle which is painful to be part of. However we are seeing, more and more, that mindfulness is a very effective tool to help with this.

Learning Some More

You can use the following sequence of questions to help you become more aware of the extent to which you use food as a friend.

Emotional Eating: Do your emotions trigger you to eat at the wrong times?

Do you turn to food when you're feeling stressed?

Do you eat when you are already quite full?

Do you reward yourself with food?

Do you regularly eat until you are stuffed full?

Does food help you feel safe?

Does food feel like a friend? Always there for you...

Do you turn away from food when you are upset by something (especially over a loss, or someone leaving)?

Do you feel powerless to control yourself around some types of food?

You can tell from the questions that the more you answered, 'yes.' the more likely it is that you are an emotional eater. This is an exciting moment as you have given yourself a piece of information which can lead to some creative, interesting changes in your behavior. Making no judgments about this information, you can stay in your mindful state and breathe into the information. Send loving, appreciative thoughts to yourself for allowing you to notice this situation. Then gently return to your mindful breathing as described by Thich Nhat Hatch …. Or look around you and observe the intensity of the blue sky, the bird sounds or the silence in the present moment. Know that all will be well as the process of mindfulness takes you through the painful bits and into healing.

Emotional Hunger

Emotional eating is something that most of us do at some time. Some do it more often and the drive to eat is felt like an insatiable hunger leading them to some compulsive behaviors. For example, have you ever suddenly felt an overwhelming desire to eat? Not only that, but it is only certain types of food you crave at that moment? It has to be that KitKat bar, it must be cheese and onion chips or Domino's pizza and a chocolate brownie from Starbucks.

 Have you also noticed that when you grab that food you bolt it down, without any thought and with little enjoyment? In fact, you often feel like you then need to have another, and another, and another…. Until you are full – but also feeling a bit sickened. This whole process has been much more in your mind – a craving – rather than hunger in your body. Along with that 'sickened' feeling at the overload of fats, oils or sugar, there is often an uncomfortable prickle of guilt or shame. That is when you begin to slide into a very vicious bout of self-talk around being a terrible person who can't control themselves, that you are fat, impossible, weak..... And so the negative, unkind judgments come pouring out, making you feel worse and worse – and worse. It's a situation many people will recognize, and it can range from happening the odd time under certain conditions – right through to being a vicious cycle that you live in on a daily basis.

Wherever you are on that continuum of emotional responses leading to compulsive eating, it is a wonderful thing that you are interested in mindfulness because this practice will help you so much to both recognize and accept how you are right now. And, strangely enough with that calm acceptance, it helps to foster in you, it will help you transform that behavior to actions that will truly show love to your body in every present moment.

Top Mindfulness Tips

1. With your developing loving kindness, you can start to notice not only the sensations of emotional hunger but also what triggered them off. These sensations usually come on very suddenly, and it is easy to miss the trigger if you are not tuning in gently and lovingly – and more frequently - to your body.

Hindsight, Midsight, Foresight.

The way this process of noticing usually works is that at first, you will be able to identify what happened in 'hindsight.' After a while of noticing after the event, you will begin to pick it up in 'mid-sight.' In other words, you will see as you reach for the chocolate brownie or the packet of chips and will be able to say to yourself, 'How interesting, this is me trying to comfort myself with food.' Or 'this is me not knowing what to do when I'm scared.'

You will be disrupting the less desirable emotional eating behavior with this awareness. Then after a time of noticing what is happening, and when, in 'mid-sight' you will begin to pick it up in 'fore-sight.' This is when you recognize that you are entering a stressful situation and that this is a time when you tend to feel more vulnerable, fearful, angry…(Or whatever emotion it is that you have been trying to manage). As soon as you recognize the situation may be about to arise, you can take new, different steps to give yourself comfort or relieve your anxiety.

You have always been trying to help yourself

An important thing to remember is that you have always been trying to look after yourself, even when your behavior wasn't very helpful. Far from being something to beat yourself up about it is something to admire about yourself. You were showing care and commitment to yourself – being very young at the time sometimes the things you chose to do weren't the most effective, but the wish to take care of yourself was there. Now you can take that innate self-love and form new habits around useful behaviors.

What a wonderful gift that will be. Thanks to mindfulness.

Chapter 5 Transforming the Cycle of Emotional Eating

"Walk as if you are kissing the Earth with your feet." – Thich Nhat Hanh

Having found out through your mindfulness practice that you are an amazingly creative person who unconsciously has been trying to comfort, support, manage and cope with situations and emotions, you can now move on with even more interest and kindness to finding out new ways to take care of yourself.

You are an intelligent person and know very well that the nutritional information you get in diets regarding calories is not the answer. You had recognized that food was your friend and supporter or your distractor from emotions you had no idea how to deal with this because you had very little help learning how to handle emotional states them when you were young. But now you are grown up and know that there are alternatives to food for friendship, support, and distraction and that emotions can be managed, even when they are challenging ones.

See if you recognize any of these emotions in yourself

Typical feelings you may have been trying to calm and contain with food are:

Loneliness

Depression

Anxiety

Exhaustion

Anger

Fear

Boredom

Very often these emotions are triggered by conflicts in one or more of your relationships or by being overwhelmed at work, or having too many roles or tasks to juggle, or financial difficulties or ongoing health problems.

Alternative Ways to Manage these Emotions

With your new creative, curious and kind approach and the regular practice of Mindful Meditation, you can begin to experiment with alternatives that appeal to you.

Loneliness and Depression

Have regular phone calls, get together's, Skype calls, postings on Facebook, texts... between you and a number of your friends. Actively keep connections alive and flourishing.

Every night before you go to sleep take the time to think back over the day and how much good contact you had with people – from the lady teller at the grocery store who chatted with you, to your friends and family, to your pets, to yourself! Take this time to be appreciative of these people or animals and feel gratitude for having them in your life.

Depression

(it is even better if you write these things down every night in a Gratitude Journal. In no time you have a record of beautiful memories and realizations that you can look at if you feel a bit down. They will soon lift your spirits.)

Take up classes in something you have been interested in for a while. These can be online classes if you can't find babysitters or make a plan to free up the time any other way. Ideally, the classes would be in something physical. Get moving somehow. Movement changes your body chemistry and anxiety, fear and anger flood you with the wrong kind of hormones, such as adrenaline and cortisol. Get these reduced and replaced by 'more helpful' hormones such as dopamine and serotonin, and you will feel like a different person.

Anxiety

Yoga is an excellent choice for this as it is a mindful practice in itself and a yoga class takes you from centering yourself in your body, through a natural stretch and strength building workout, right through to calm, conscious relaxation where you let yourself completely relax and let go as the floor supports you. All kinds of 'good' biochemicals are released through this practice.

Anger and Fear

A great alternative is dancing. This can be anything from dancing with the mop as you sweep the yard or the floor, to boogying to some badass music you switch on when you're alone to joining a dance class or going to a night club. Some great resources for this are online from all the music on iTunes and YouTube to the 5 Rhythm's freestyle dancing of Gabrielle Roth to local ballroom dancing classes. Find your dancing delight and get dancing.

Exhaustion

Fatigue can have many causes so it is always worth having a medical check up. However while you do that you can get started with loving, compassionate kindness to your tired Self by:

- Sitting down between tasks (or standing up and doing some deep breathing at the window if your job is sedentary),
- Making sure you don't miss breakfast or lunch,
- Taking a cat nap every day (5 minutes is enough to pick you up – 20 mins is ideal).
- Taking a very relaxing bath every day, use essential oils and soak tiredness away in quiet candle light
- Notice times when you can sit rather than stand, lean, rather than pace, lie rather than sit!
- Literally, put your feet up whenever you can to rest your heart and allow any excess fluid to drain away.
- Regularly give yourself the pleasure of the yoga posture called 'legs up the wall.' Here you lie on the floor (on a blanket, carpet, or soft mat) and swing your legs up until they are resting against the wall. It is even more comfortable if you lift up your pelvis and tuck a pillow under your buttocks. Rest quietly here for 5 minutes or more in your lunch break and you will find yourself recharged for the afternoon.
- Change you tea or coffee drinking to using herbal teas at least some of the time. Chamomile tea at nighttime is lovely to help you sleep more peacefully. During the day just

sipping at a refreshing herbal tea such as rosehip or rooibos which has a teaspoon of honey in it is calming and comforting.

<u>Boredom</u>

Boredom can be challenging as preparing and eating food is a common way to structure time and give you something to do. Using your mindfulness to notice that boredom is a familiar feeling you have is very helpful as it can lead to questions about what there is too little of in your life. In turn, this can help you work out lifestyle changes and finding the fulfillment you really want in your life. This questioning is the start of another fascinating journey of self-discovery and can be undertaken with a counselor, therapist, journal, trusted a friend or whatever support you sense might help. It can be the start of a new life.

Top Mindfulness Tips

- Drink more water. Mindfully place your jug of filtered or spa water in the sunlight for a few hours so that it can absorb the beauty of the sun's rays. When you drink it feel the sun's goodness soaking into your body.
- Chew for longer so that the first stage of digestion is well underway before the food slides down to your tummy. Chewing helps not only to break down the food and make it easier to absorb from, but also exercises the jaw muscles, teeth, and gums. It releases flavors and gives us time for every 'layer' of taste, texture and aroma to be freed as the food moves from the front of the tongue to the back. As we have different taste sensors in various sections of our tongue, we only notice the richness of the taste experience as each part becomes activated – sweet, sour, salt, bitter… The complexity and interest of the food becomes greater the more we chew.
- Get yourself to bed nice and early. Or, at the very least, make sure you have enough sleep. Fatigue stimulates appetite as an attempt to boost metabolism and get more energy so it is a good idea to make rest and sleep a priority. As a bonus, a rested body can more easily settle to meditation and mindfulness as there is less agitation in your system, making that 'mind monkey.' less hyperactive!

- Take 'regular' and 'balanced' as your watchwords for eating. Regular, balanced meals with the right combination of protein, carbohydrates, and fats in them work like magic on our bodies. The more the habit of mindfulness becomes part of who you are the more you will tune to your body and notice that the peaks and troughs of energy and moods you lived with become things of the past as your body settles to a steady combustion of readily available nutrients. Your life begins to reflect a more natural flow of energy, activity and rest.

Chapter 6 - Mindful Eating in a Mindful Life

"People usually consider walking on water or in thin air a miracle. But I think the real miracle is not to walk either on water or in thin air, but to walk on earth. Every day we are engaged in a miracle which we don't even recognize: a blue sky, white clouds, green leaves, the black, curious eyes of a child — our own two eyes. All is a miracle." — Thich Nhat Hanh. Every day is a Miracle

As the practice of mindfulness becomes an easy and integral part of your everyday life you will find more and more to be appreciative of in the world and in yourself. Although it is such a simple practice Mindfulness has the power to transform our lives, or part of our lives, such as the relationship with food. It also brings the gift of more joy, more love, more happiness to our lives. From being trapped in a flat, somewhat negative, anxious or agitated state which has absorbed our attention, energy and awareness for so long, it changes us. We become able to lift ourselves out of the 'flatness' and the unhelpful absorption as we tune into the trees, the air, our breath, our sensations, the wonder of other human beings. Something amazing seems to happen to our hearts too as we feel the gratitude and appreciation we now practice daily softening our hearts. The capacity to give and accept love grows and our lives flourish and grow rich.

It can seem like a miracle that a commitment to a simple practice like this can bring about such changes – but it can. Your only task is to stick with it and allow the process of mindfulness unfold you. In a short time, it will be automatic to approach your food in this spirit and here are some more suggestions for doing that.

Mindful Eating

Mindful eating starts when you shop! Or maybe even before that as you plan for what you will be eating during the week or the day.

<u>Planning</u>

It used to be the case that families shopped daily and routinely bought what was fresh and in season. They would also tend to get it from local sources, making it an even healthier choice for themselves – and the planet. This is less realistic these days, although farmers markets have helped to make a Saturday trip a pleasure to look forward to.

Take time to plan as a family if you have one, or if you are single make it a pleasurable activity to think this through. Think of what is fresh and in season, consult your inner 'Gourmet' to find out what he/she is drawn to, at this time, scan your memory for dishes you have enjoyed in the past... If you like doing internet research, this is a wonderful excuse to spend time looking at recipes, finding ideas on health and food sites and creating master lists to make your shopping easier. Many of the large food retailers have their own sites with pre-filled master-lists. They do it to encourage you to use their online ordering service – but you can benefit from their work by using the master lists and adapting them for your home use.

It can be tempting – and practical – to use the home delivery service but be aware that you miss the joy of checking out the fresh produce with the unique textures, smells, and visuals. A good compromise can be to order dried, tinned or boxed products from them online – but make an expedition to somewhere local to source fruits and vegetables with your own hands and eyes and nose.

When you shop

Don't go when you are hungry – a fatal way to sabotage the whole experience!

Build up relationships with the people selling the produce/products. Even in supermarkets, this is possible, and it makes the experience of shopping far more pleasurable. Short conversation, a warm smile, a nod of recognition all contribute to making the time spent there richer. Who knows they may start to make sure you know about the specials or when fresh new produce is brought in.

We tend to push in a shopping trip as a chore but with a mindful approach, we can 'stop' and rethink this way of doing it. And we can turn it into a very different experience, which still doesn't need to take much time, but our mindful radars will be attuned to gratitude, kindness and appreciation as well as good prices and good food as we shop. Try it – it's fun.

Preparing the food

Before you begin to prepare the food put the ingredients you need out on the counter and take a mindful moment to really see them. Pick up the fresh vegetables, fruit, meat and smell them, touch them and see the subtleties of shape, color, and patterning before you begin to chop and cook.

It is also a lovely practice to bless the food as you prepare it. That loving energy seems to flow into the meal and add a unique quality to its goodness.

The last part of the preparing phase is to do with visual presentation. The Japanese are masters of this art, and it is something that you might enjoy as you plate the food for serving. Think less is more, let the shapes and colors of the food speak for themselves and not be too overwhelmed by each other by being crowded on the plate. Even it the plate is just for you think about what you would like to see if it were put down in front of you at a restaurant. Why not make it like that for yourself!

<u>Eating the food</u>

A recent survey showed that typically families only eat together once a week these days. Understandable in the rush of living at the moment but not good for relationships and health.

If it is possible to encourage the family to sit down together more often, that will help. If that isn't possible the make the most of the times when everyone is together.

Take time to turn off the computer, the TV, the radio, mobile…. Commit to half an hour (or whatever works for you) of sharing the food and each other's company.

Come to the table with a physical appetite. Make the food available when people are likely to be ready for it physically, not just as a break from the routine.

If it is a comfortable practice in the home take the time to bless the food, and each other, as you start.

Encourage the others to 'stop' and mindfully be aware of what is on the plate before tucking in. Give that mindful moment to enjoying the aroma, the textures, the colors – then eat with relish.

Take enough time to chew the food thoroughly. Take note of the section earlier in the document regarding taste, flavor and chewing. However, you can extend the practice even more by taking smaller bites. More flavor will unpack itself as you chew and the message from your tummy, when it is full, will come through more clearly because you are eating more slowly.

Play a game with the food which will help you focus even more on the flavor. Try to guess/taste what you are eating and each of the ingredients. It's fun to do and is bound to please the cook to have that much attention paid to the food.

A radical change for people eating together would be to experiment with silence! Save the chat until after the food is eaten, or at least until the first course is eaten. There is something about eating in silence that enhances every part of the experience. It allows you to slow down, really attend to the food, to ingest and digest all the goodness in the dish and to realize the extraordinary number of people and processes that went into getting this meal on the table just for you. It's humbling! Once the first pangs of physical hunger are taken care of with silence chatting can start, but it is likely to be a richer conversation for having had that quiet time. Try it and see! Of course, if you are eating alone silence is easy, but remember to switch off the TV before you sit down.

Mindful eating enables you to notice when you are full enough. We often miss this moment through agitation, rushing and not paying attention to our body signals. Also, naughtily, food manufacturers of processed food slip in extra salt, sugar, fats or MSG to encourage us to eat more. All of these substances have an addictive aspect and without mindfulness, it is easy to get hooked into feeling that you need more to be satisfied.

<u>After eating</u>
If you do feel like you need another plateful and that feeling is not based on having done a lot of physical exercise recently give yourself 20 minutes digestion time and then ask yourself again if you need that extra plateful. Twenty minutes makes a big difference to the signals coming from our bodies. If your body still says 'YES" then have another plateful. Enjoy it thoroughly.

If you are using mindful eating as part of a weight management program, make a note of anything you became aware of as you ate. Did you have any non-hunger triggers going on during the meal or before? Where you physically hungry when you came to the table? Which ingredients in the meal did you really enjoy this time? What made a difference to your pleasure and attention as you ate?

Take another mindful moment to appreciate yourself for your commitment to your own health and happiness.

Best Mindful Tip

"The present moment is filled with joy and happiness. If you are attentive, you will see it." Thich Nhat Hanh

Chapter 7 - Mindfulness and Health

Many of the Mindfulness tips are very effective ways to enhance your health as well and deepen your mindfulness practice. The most important of these is definitely to ....

SLOOOOOW Down.......

In a stressful world where many people having high anxiety levels as they live in the future – worrying what will happen to situations they cannot control – the pace of life seems to get faster and faster. Given that what most people really, really want when they are asked is simply to 'be happy' living a life of future focused anxiety or past focused worry will not give them much happiness. The great gift of Mindfulness is that it can be the pathway to a far happier life as you live more of more of the time in the present which is FULL of things to appreciate and be happy about when one slows down enough to engage with this moment.

What Else will Help to Boost Both yourHealth and your Mindfulness?

Linked to slowing down is another important step towards greater happiness which is 'Stepping back'.

<u>Stepping back</u>

Stepping back means re-evaluating what is bringing you the things you want – including happy moments and joy. This can lead to a change in life direction because the work you do brings so little happiness to you – or to a decision to do less as you recognize what can be weeded out to focus more time on the joyful parts of your life.

It can also mean a change in your behavior as you change the 'butterfly approach' so common amongst anxious, worrying people where you flit from task to task constantly, doing none of them very accurately or efficiently. Stepping back to re-evaluate can mean that you begin to just focus on one task at a time, and finish it. This can feel more satisfying and help you appreciate yourself more deeply at the end of a productive day.

<u>Planning your time</u>

Having a schedule is calming! Even for people who like variety and spontaneity! You just have to schedule the variety and 'mad moments' time in. Our bodies work better in a life of regularity – or at least having enough of our time, energy, body and brain doing the same things at the same time. It helps us feel more secure, and it helps our bodies function healthily – the trick is to work out how much 'enough' scheduling is right for you. The more mindful you are, the more you can pick up the signals from your body and your mind about what they need regarding regular input and output.

Finding someone to talk to

Slowing down and being mindful can bring about more, and deeper, insights – and it really helps to have someone to chat these over with. A good friend is great, or a counselor is also an excellent choice as they will listen to you non-judgmentally and not attempt to sway you in any particular direction. They will just listen. Keeping a journal is an option that works for many – a safe place to write things down and make sense out of the insights you are having about what is existing in every moment. In fact, the very best option is to keep a journal AND have someone else to chat to.

Disconnect!

In all possible ways! Disconnect your mobile, your laptop, your PC, your iPad. Yes, really! Just for a short time while your brain clears of electronic jumble and you pat attention to something else. That something else may be the view, the dog, your child, your partner, yourself. It doesn't matter what it is – it's just that your brain needs a break. Give yourself an 'Unhooked Half Hour'/day. And as usual, observe how you respond to that. You can always change if that doesn't suit you.

You can make even more of this disconnected time by being mindful of your breathing. Just focusing in on breath in, pause, breath out, pause, gives you downtime and enables your nervous system to quieten down. Bliss! You need a minimum of twenty minutes for this to help the biochemical soup in your brain and body to change to a better mixture.

<u>Focus on Folk</u>

How often have you spent time with someone, chatted away with them, had a meeting with them, even had a meal with them – only to find that afterward, you realize that you hardly remember what was said or how they were. In other words, you weren't actually there fully. There in body – but not in mind! You might have been thinking of what you have to do next. You may have been thinking of what you need to cook that night, what you were worrying about at that time, or how you going to fit in time to write that report.

A whole conversation may have passed you by – and this may happen often. Best practice is to give yourself 2 minutes before meeting up with the person to shift your attention to them and what the conversation will be about and/or the pleasure you will get from being with this person, and away from what you are doing. Think of three things about them that you really appreciate so that you begin to tune into the positive before you even get together.

It takes a bit of effort initially to be fully present but the quality of every single conversation, meeting and relationship will change for the better if you do this. Have a go and then mindfully reflect on the results. This is a true connection, and it is something we are wired to do for our mental health.

Learn New Productivity Habits

There are many helpful hacks on the web now with good advice on how to make the most of the time you have. Many you will know and probably use most of them. However, there are likely to be some you haven't heard of. Any small tip you can pick up to simplify your life and create more space while increasing your efficiency makes sense to do. A simple one I have found handy is to be realistic about what can be accomplished in a day. Don't timetable more than 5 tasks, and of those tasks make only one or two of them big tasks. Another helpful tip taught me to timetable in 'unexpected time'. This means that there is wriggle room in your diary to deal with the unexpected dramas, traumas or crises that inevitably crop up. Getting to the end of a day where there has been enough time for each task means you are far calmer going home or turning to the next part of your day with some energy left for being mindful in the new situation.

Saying 'No' Mindfully

Linked to all the above is the skill of 'saying, No'. Being assertive about managing our valuable time and energy is an obvious advantage. However, saying 'no' mindfully brings in another dimension. Your body is FULL of cues and clues for what is good for it and what is not. But we often miss these hints as we are so busy either reacting blindly by saying 'yes', or by rebelling loudly by saying 'NO'! saying to someone who is asking something of you needs a more mindful approach to be successful. This means always saying kindly, 'Let me come back to you about that.'before you say either 'yes' or 'no.'

It allows you to run the request through both your mind and your body, breathing into both as you mindfully focus on what is going on in the present moment internally. You may then hear the deep sigh your body heaves as it 'thinks' of taking on an extra task, staying on late at work, missing that yoga class again. That's a sign of tired resignation – your body doesn't really want to do this. You may also feel a funny sinking of your heart, a churning of your tummy…. All cues and clues from your body that it would be better not to take this one on.

Alternatively, your body may heave an enormous sigh of relief as it says 'YES' to the request. Your body likes the idea a lot and is excited about it. That is another big clue as to what to do. It may then mean that you fit this new request into your timetable – and drop something else that your body not like as much! Remember you can always go back to someone to re-negotiate what was initially agreed.

This brings us to another vital tip for STOPPING.

<u>You Can Change Your Mind</u>

Part of making our lives be so clogged up with 'things to do' comes from believing that w have to stick to what we have said no matter what. It can be an enormous relief to see the reminder that that is not true! In fact, it is a good thing to have an open and flexible enough mind to rethink something and change your original decision. The challenge can sometimes be to negotiate with someone else about this change. However, if you go into the negotiation in plenty of time and have a mindset that works towards a new outcome that will be good enough for each party – you may even come up with a better plan than the original one! So much changes all the time that your re-negotiation may work far better because some key factors have changed in the meantime.

Stopping At Each Transition Point in Your Day

One thing that many of us are poor at doing is taking the time to 'finish' the business we are engaged with at the moment, withdrawing and then centering before going n to the next task or event of the day.

 The biggest transition of the day can be the one between 'working' and 'going home'. This journey, or transition, can be done so gracefully and mindfully that it will become an important feature of your life. Taking time to organize your documents, tidy your workspace, clear the loose ends by just writing them down for the to do list tomorrow can be remarkably helpful in clearing your head of the day gone by and making it fresh and open for the present moment and whatever that is bringing as you change focus.

Another way of putting this is 'Don't take your work home with you'. Don't worry about something coming up tomorrow – just be in the flow of your life – lightly letting go of what has been, engaging with what is and leaving the future to unfold as it may.

This leads us to the last mindful tip....

<u>Know That You Are a Creative, Resilient Person</u>

You must be to have got to where you are now! Negotiating a life these days is a constant creative, cooperative adventure and you've made it work for you up to this point. This is enough to allow you to relax about tomorrow. Life will not stop bringing you a stream of challenges and joys in an entirely random mixture. What you can do now as you step back is recognize that you have negotiated all the rapids and calm pools, and that very few of them were things you had been expecting. Life is just like that. The one common center has always been YOU; creative, inventive, you making it up as you go along, finding a way around, through and over whatever has come your way. This means that you can be confident in yourself that you will continue to be this creative and resilient no matter what life brings – so there is absolutely no point in worrying about what tomorrow will bring. You can be sure that you will be able to deal with it. With your mindful practice, you will also be able to appreciate yourself and many new aspects of every situation than ever before. This is one of the many ways Mindfulness can transform your life.

There are so many good things we can be doing to help ourselves and our health – and then doing each of them mindfully - that this in itself becomes a demand and feels overwhelming. If this is how you feel as you read through the tips and ideas step back, take a breath and remind yourself that there is time. Just choose one thing to focus on quietly and steadily, whenever you have your mindfulness time and leave ALL the other's alone/.

Chapter 8- Living the Mindful Life

The further into each present moment you enter, the more you discover to notice and appreciate!

If you find yourself responding to the idea of 'mindfulness' and are sensing just how much richness, pleasure, and steadiness it can bring you daily, you might find that you begin expanding your concept of mindfulness to take in other aspects of your life

Being mindful about the origin of your food

Since we have been focusing on mindful eating the next step you take could be to notice how close to its natural state the food you are eating is. There is a lot of scaremongering about the dangers of processed food as the cause of the obesity epidemic in the western world. Sometimes it is hard to unpick what is accurate and what is sensational.

However, we do know that cultures which eat very directly from the land with as little cooking as possible tend to have longer lives and be less prone to many of the chronic diseases we suffer from in the West. So, without being fanatical about it and just taking a 'curious' approach, you can begin to observe three fascinating things.

1. How close to nature is this food?
2. Who and what has enabled me to be preparing/eating this food right now?
3. How do I feel when I eat this compared to how I feel if the food is processed?

As you begin to choose and handle the food to prepare it, your mindfulness practice will bring your imagination to life. You can conjure up a colorful picture story of the vegetables growing, being picked by the farmer, being packaged and then being driven by a person traveling on safely constructed roads to the store or distribution center. Even going beyond that you can picture ad appreciate the people and systems involved in organizing, pricing and displaying the goods in the place you are shopping.

The more you enter into the present moment, the more you realize that the produce you have in your hands is the result of an extraordinary network of cooperation between human beings and nature. You can then have fun in comparing the experience of buying your food either directly from the producers, such as through local farmers markets or small stores, or from a supermarket or from a drive-through fast food outlet. Each has their own incredible network of human cooperation involved, and each has a richness to be experienced. Your only job is to observe, with loving kindness, which gives you the most satisfying time.

Taking it a little further

Appreciating the wonderful cooperative networks and systems which combine to bring food to your hands is an exciting part of mindfulness – but it might also start you on a journey to grow your own foods! There is very little as fulfilling as picking those vegetables straight from the ground, plucking the fruit straight from the trees and preparing a meal with your own organic, free range eggs. The joy of knowing you are eating very health-supporting foods, caring for yourself and the family and being part of a cooperative process with Nature herself takes some beating.

Of course, not everyone is in a situation where this is possible, thinking of those of you living in flats or homes without yards. It is still possible to grow herbs indoors and that alone is a joy as you flavor your dishes with homegrown goodness. If that is not something that appeals you may find some friends or family members who do like to do it and ask them to share with you. It just adds to the whole mindful moment when you put the first forkful in your mouth.

Mindful eating and the Planet

Anything that links with Nature immediately takes us to the greater perspective of the Planet itself. And from there it is one small step to considering the carbon footprint the food you are eating is leaving on the world. Lovely as it is to be able to access out of season food throughout the year it does have an impact on the atmosphere we breathe. As the atmosphere changes global warming becomes more of an issue and ecosystems all over the planet; from the oceans to the soil, are affected.

It can be humbling to begin to be mindful of some much, and so many issues, surrounding the food we eat. You can, of course, chose how much of this to be aware of and how much you may, or may not, change your behavior as a result. Remembering that Mindfulness is a non-judgmental practice, based on curiosity and compassion, whatever you take out of it is right for you and does not need to be 'right' for anyone else. This is YOUR practice.

Conclusion

If you enjoyed this book and found something to experiment with, try out, share or commit to we are delighted.

Health and happiness can be found through many avenues and for all of them the journey itself is usually the joy. The destination is what we want to achieve, but it is in getting there that we constantly find out more about ourselves and our own uniqueness. And this is the most fascinating of all.

Until we meet again in another book – be healthy, be happy, be beautiful inside and out.

Sending you lots of love from here,

Maya Faro

For similar wellness, health & spirituality books, visit:

www.YourWellnessBooks.com

and

www.LOAforSuccess.com

www.ingramcontent.com/pod-product-compliance
Lightning Source LLC
Chambersburg PA
CBHW042121100526
44587CB00025B/4139